ENDORSEM

If I could give one book to struggling C[...]
Tammaney Holcombe packs a lot of helpful and practical biblical principles for parenting into this short read, which are so valuable for raising children in today's world. With all the conflicting advice out there, many mothers are confused about how to bring up kids to know and love Christ, but Miss Tammaney's Quips and Tidbits cuts right to the heart of the matter: we must parent based on God's Word, His design and solid foundation.

—Marisa Boonstra, Founder of Called To Mothering

TESTIMONIALS

I have always felt like I was a well-educated person. My husband and I were older than typical parents, so we were also somewhat "well educated" in life. I have younger nieces and nephews that I felt like I was being a good role model for and helping give advice that would grow them into well rounded individuals. I mean, after all, I had a bachelor's degree in early childhood education, a master's in elementary education, and an educational specialist degree in instructional technology. I have taught children from primary age all the way up to high school. I should have known what to do to raise my own child. Wrong! I questioned everything that I did! Miss Tammaney gave me and is still giving me an education about raising my child way more than any degree. She is definitely a blessing!

—Greta Hughes

I believe the most significant thing about Miss Tammaney is that she loves with her whole being. Her actions display the summarization of her advice. Be present. Listen. Be honest. Listen. Love. Laugh. Listen to music that uplifts you. Surround yourself with things of art—God made and made from those He gives a talent to. Love. Love others more than yourself. I believe her best advice is her life. She is a child of the King, whom she loves and serves without reservation or borders. She loves her husband and girls the way all wives and moms should love their families. Miss Tammaney loves strangers the way Christ calls us to love. She is a friend who is there no matter what. She is a teacher who loves to inspire and make "her kids," (students) think way beyond the surface. She is a teacher who becomes a friend and a role model to the kids who have grown up. I can't think of a better way to live than for your life to speak for itself.

—Stacy Cook

Miss Tammaney encouraged me as a parent about the importance of having a village. "Once they are grown, you still need that village. Sometimes members come and go depending on the age and stages of the child, but you will appreciate that village as the child ages. One's church is a great foundational village. Be protective over this village."

—Summer Erikson

Miss Tammaney was an encourager for me. "Over praising is not good for a child. Don't give your child a compliment unless it is deserved." I think by following her advice, my children have developed a healthy sense of self. I love how she is not afraid to speak the truth in love.

—Amy Holmes

A specific impact that occurred for us was when Miss Tammaney coached us about transitions. "Give your child a warning or heads up when you are ready for them to switch gears. This makes for better, smoother transitions." We still do this and find that it makes our parenting much more harmonious. Giving Pip a little verbal warning was a parenting paradigm shift for us that led to fewer tears, shouts, fits, and hysterics.

—Lisa & Chad McKinney

When I was melancholy about my children growing up, I learned to "embrace the stage" as Miss Tammaney said to me. "When you are present in the moment, you won't miss what's happening because you are trying to keep them young or make them grow up too fast." I learned to reap the rewards in all stages of my children's lives.

—Carla Conduff

Miss Tammaney tells me, "It's not the end of the world if you mess up. Try, try again!" I know she loves me because she and Mr. David came to my baptism. That made me so happy that something burst inside my heart. Now I know she has a special place in my heart!

—Naomi Dixon, age 8

Miss Tammaney once told me when I was worried about Kiley being too bossy that Kiley was "not bossy, but a leader." That comment has stayed with me. She loved and nurtured my babies when I was so worried about them starting school. She expected them to be independent and taught them how, but she did it with love. My children adored her then and they still do as teenagers.

—Shelly Abernathy

I could write a book myself with the ways Miss Tammaney has impacted me as a mom, wife, and teacher. Specific advice we received from her was about the importance of making our marriage a priority, fostering creativity, discipline, putting God first, and being open with our kids.

—Brian & Eve Priest

My son had issues with his emotions when he was young. Melt downs, kicking and screaming, and crying was a common scene. Once other people experienced this behavior in him, we were excluded in birthday invitations, social gatherings, and even church attendance. We were at a loss. No one knew how I prayed every night for answers, that I had sought out help from the pediatrician, and just about every self-help book I could find. Miss Tammaney didn't know this either when we walked into the children's church class for the first time. After a few weeks of attending here, it happened! The dreaded meltdown! He was in full blown meltdown mode and I opened the door to grab him and escape and was stopped by Miss Tammaney. She simply said, "It's ok. I can handle this" and closed the door. I honestly had no idea how to respond. So I waited. Once the screaming stopped (not as long as normal) and the children were released, Miss Tammaney came to me and told me all about the fun that had occurred in class, and how he had had a moment but that he was learning how to express his emotions. And then with a smile she said, "See you next week!" For weeks I received that kind of encouragement. She was very patient and quiet with him as he learned how to handle his own emotions all the while teaching me how to model that as well. She taught me to see him differently and lead him to do the same. Each week, we felt safe in her care. Our son had not only gained the tools for controlling his emotions, but he learned to communicate them himself in a manner that helped others to see his heart. He learned the Bible and was attentive in class. As a parent, this was immeasurable for me. We finally found a church we could attend that was not afraid of his big emotions and where they welcomed us all with love. I really cannot put into words how much her guidance and simple love for my son filled my heart and soul. It was a blessing beyond measure to know that my son was loved beyond measure and to know that someone saw who he was inside. My son also knew this and was always happy to go to class.

—Candi Phillips

As a family, we were discussing Mr. Rogers and A Beautiful Day in the Neighborhood movie. One of my eleven-year-old twin sons, Connor, asked, "Who is Mr. Rogers?" Harper's response was so quick and matter of fact. She explained in her precocious six-year-old voice, "Mr. Rogers is just like my Miss Tammaney. Really, she is a 'girl Mr. Rogers.'" She went on telling him that both are teachers, both love kids very much, and both love books and activities. After watching the movie, Connor said, "Harper, you're right! She is a 'girl Mr. Rogers.'" Harper said, "Well, duh! I know!"

—Ashley Moore

Miss Tammaney's
QUIPS & TIDBITS

Miss Tammaney's
QUIPS & TIDBITS

REDEMPTION PRESS

Published by Redemption Press, PO Box 427, Enumclaw, WA 98022.
Toll-Free (844) 2REDEEM (273-3336)

Redemption Press is honored to present this title in partnership with the author. The views expressed or implied in this work are those of the author. Redemption Press provides our imprint seal representing design excellence, creative content, and high-quality production.

ISBN 13: 978-1-64645-514-0 (Paperback)

Library of Congress Catalog Card Number: 2021915095

DEDICATION

This book is dedicated to my husband, David and to my daughters, Malloree and Courtney. God used their lives to interrupt my life. Those positive ripples of change have impacted the lives of many. If these "quips and tidbits" can improve the life of one more, all the learning and painful growth I experienced was worth it. To God be the glory!

ACKNOWLEDGEMENTS

First, I would like to thank God for the redemption of my life through the blood of Jesus Christ. I am grateful to God for creating The P.L.A.Y. House. He had a plan I never dreamed of. I thank my family for their endurance and support in my many adventures. Thanks to all the children who have taught me over the years, and to their parents for their transparency and authenticity. An extra-big thank-you to parents who contributed to this book. I'm grateful to Kara Clay and Hannah Dearman for artwork and assistance. My intimate prayer team, Angie, Chrissy, Debbie, Donna, Missy, and Lisa have held me up and kept me going through the process. Enormous thanks to Miss Paula for continually encouraging me to write these quips down for others. To God be the glory!

CONTENTS

PREFACE

I am a child of God, wife, mother, teacher, and student and am privileged that several of my roles collided and enabled me to add author to that list.

With thirty-plus years of parenting experience and forty years of teaching experience, along with my passion for and continued study of both the Bible and of child development information, God has given me unique insight into training up children. I love children and have a drive for studying how their brains work, and, in turn, being intentional about what goes into their minds.

I have run a respected teaching studio that includes preschool/pre-K and Kindermusik classes for the last 21 years, and prior to that, I taught music, art, and gifted programs in both public and private schools in grades pre-K through high school at various times. Currently, I work with both parents and children—newborns through early childhood. Through my involvement with Kindermusik, I learned that home is the first learning environment for children, and parents are their first teachers. I use that philosophy in all of my teaching as well, so that I not only teach children but also provide parents with a library of resources and information they can check out to assist them in their greatest and most challenging endeavor ever—parenting.

I have offered a lot of parenting advice over the years, when I have been asked. To my surprise, I have had many parents suggest I write a book with my parenting tidbits and quips. One parent, in particular, was insistent, so I agreed to pray about it, never imagining God would confirm I was meant to take on such an undertaking. God's plans, however, are not always our plans, so when He spoke and confirmed this book, I obeyed. I expect obedience from my preschoolers, so I figured I should obey too!

Just as I pray for my students and my potential students and their parents, I am also praying for you and your kids. I pray that this book will be a blessing to your family.

INTRODUCTION

This book is written from my heart–a heart that desires to see moms and dads lead young children in a way that guides them to becoming followers of Jesus in adulthood. These children who God has entrusted into our care are always taking in information. As parents, we are called to a higher level of thinking and awareness, so that we are mindful of what we are pouring into our children. Perfection is not the goal—it is unattainable for our kids and for us as parents. Our goal is to lead our kids to a lifelong relationship with Jesus. Through this book, I hope to inspire you to lead them to Jesus and to be authentic, aware, and intentional with your parenting, practicing grace each step of the way with ourselves and with our children.

These words that God gave Moses in Deuteronomy have provided me direction in my everyday life, in my parenting, in my teaching, and are the basis of the principles in this book.

> These are the commands, decrees and laws the LORD your God directed me to teach you to observe in the land that you are crossing the Jordan to possess, so that you, your children and their children after them may fear the LORD your God as long as you live by keeping all his decrees and commands that I give you, and so that you may enjoy long life. Hear, Israel, and be careful to obey so that it may go well with you and that you may increase greatly in a land flowing with milk and honey, just as the LORD, the God of your ancestors, promised you.
>
> Hear, O Israel: The LORD our God, the LORD is one. Love the LORD your God with all your heart and with all your soul and with all your strength. These commandments that I give you today are to be upon your hearts. Impress them on

your children. Talk about them when you sit at home and when you walk along the road, when you lie down and when you get up. Tie them as symbols on your hands and bind them on your foreheads. Write them on the doorframes of your houses and on your gates. (Deuteronomy 6:1–9)

This Scripture was especially encouraging to me as God overhauled my life and brought me under authority to Him. It gave me hope for myself and also for my daughters, inspiring me to teach, lead, and demonstrate loving the Lord with all my heart, soul, and strength. I've tried to model this in my parenting and in my teaching.

After going through a divorce as a young adult, I finally realized I needed a Savior. I needed Jesus and a total surrendering to His lordship. It did not occur overnight, but I knew within my heart that I was not self-sufficient and only He could clean me up. I began a committed life with Jesus, and He transformed my life. I praise God that I had His direction to rely on when parenting my two daughters, now in their thirties, and in speaking into the lives of the littles ones I continue to teach.

I pray you find comfort knowing you are not self-sufficient and that God is there for you in every aspect of your life, including parenting. This book is not a replacement for God's Word, rather it is based on the principles the Bible provides. Jesus and God's Word are the ultimate guide for parenting. The Holy Spirit will be your Helper as you navigate this journey.

This book is organized by tidbits of advice for parents and easy to remember quips to teach children. These short sayings are easy for kids to understand and remember when they hear them repeatedly. Each quip is a nugget that stems from a much larger biblical principle, and these principles resonate with God's view of the hierarchy of the home and the role of parents within the home. I've also provided examples, explanations, and experiences to validate each quip and to help provide you with intentional strategies for leading with biblical authority. You will read stories from my life and from parents of the children I have taught, illustrating how these strategies have worked for me and for others. I pray that these testimonies will be helpful for you as well.

Biblical Principle
SUBMISSION

Parent Tidbit: Get off the fence and lead with confidence.

Quip: "Because I said so."

Remind the people to be subject to rulers and authorities, to be obedient, to be ready to do whatever is good.

Titus 3:1

You are the parent! Though they may not realize it, your children need a leader. Ask yourself if you are leading the child, or is the child leading you? Our position as parents necessitates that we are the decision makers, the leaders, the ones in charge. There must be a hierarchy of importance so that children know who is responsible. This takes the pressure off children so they know they are not responsible. You might think that is silly. Why would a child think that he or she is responsible? In my experience, when children rule the roost and make their own decisions, it sends a signal to their subconscious that they are responsible, and it can create unhealthy effects into adulthood. In his work, James Lehman developed foundational parenting programs, and his articles are very insightful. One such article, "My child thinks he's the boss!" is spot-on with regards to parental leadership. Check out his work at www.empoweringparents.com. Another valuable resource that I resonate with is John Rosemond. I began reading his parenting articles in our newspaper and started following him through his website. He has a no-nonsense approach, and some would say very old fashioned; however, his advice reflects biblical principles as well. His website is www.rosemond.com. He often uses the phrase, "Because

I said so!" in his column titles. He offers webinars and classes to parents who are looking for a real and effective way to lead their children. One of his sayings is, "The teaching of the 'Three R's' (Respect, Responsibility, and Resourcefulness) begins at home."

God designed us all to be under authority. We are under our governing authority, the authority of our bosses and leaders, and ultimately we are all under the authority of God. Romans 13:1 says, "Let everyone be subject to the governing authorities, for there is no authority except that which God has established. The authorities that exist have been established by God." Authority was created by God, and His design is best.

Do not be afraid to embrace your role as the one in charge. I am surprised at how often I hear parents ask their children if they want to obey. "Do you want to get ready to go?" "Are you ready to get your PJs on and get ready for bed?" Remember, God selected you to be your child's parent and to be responsible for guiding and instructing.

When toddlers' emotional development matures to the point they begin to recognize they have a voice and can govern their own body, it is imperative that they already have been made aware of the authority figure—you! Establishing authority from the beginning increases the likelihood of smoother sailing in the later years.

When children have the governing power in the family, it's like the tail wagging the dog. It doesn't work because children cannot make wise decisions for the family. It all starts so seemingly innocent: the child is doted upon and told how fabulous, great, and perfect they are, which builds up their ego in a manner that makes them realize their voice carries weight and control. They decide the restaurants, meals, vacations, or other decisions that affect the whole family. As they go through various emotional stages of development, which naturally brings about a desire for more independence, their ego gets too big, and they begin to rebel and pitch fits, leaving parents confused as to why their compliant child has done a 180 degree turn. Naturally, different kids' personalities handle ego differently, with some kids rebelling more than others. But God designed parents to be in charge and for all children to respect authority.

How do you establish that you are in charge so that you can properly guide and instruct your child? Boundaries. Boundaries are the basic rules and principles that you hold firm to, that will not be crossed, and that won't change. In my opinion, these need to be few but carry a lot of weight, implemented in love and guided by physical, emotional, and spiritual safety. Boundaries must be implemented when children are young and maintained consistently and persistently. (You will read more about this in the next two chapters.)

And contrary to a widespread theory, you *do not* owe a young child an explanation or a reason for those boundaries. You have established yourself as authority, so "Because I said so" is enough of an explanation with no need for discussion. You do not want to open yourself up to back and forth conversations with your child, which will lead them to believing they are in charge. As authority is established and respected and as your children mature, you can then begin pointing out the reason for the boundary.

When you tell your child that you believe you are doing what God has commanded you to do, it shows them that you are submitting to a higher authority, that you have a plan, that you are reading His Word, and that you are held accountable. At the same time, you are pointing them to Him, to His Word, and ultimately to submission.

Your most important work is your leadership as a parent. A leader shows respect yet expects obedience. A leader shows compassion but is not afraid of rules with consequences and punishment. A leader is confident in the source of his/her strength.

Part of teaching your child the hierarchy of authority includes teaching and demanding respect. "Children, obey your parents in the Lord, for this is right. 'Honor your father and mother'—which is the first commandment with a promise—'so that it may go well with you and that you may enjoy long life on the earth'" (Ephesians 6:1–3). When your children are young, honoring means accepting that you are their authority figure, obeying you, and speaking respectfully to you. Respect and obedience go hand in hand: when children respect the authority figures, they obey.

In turn, we should respect our children, treating them as special gifts from God, while guiding them in His ways. "Fathers, do not exasperate your children; instead, bring them up in the training and instruction of the Lord" (Ephesians 6:4).

"If you don't learn to do what I tell you to do, you'll never learn to do what God tells you to do." I am sure my children have heard me say this more times than they can count. In my opinion, the way we, as parents approach authority plays a huge role in the happiness of our children as adults. When I became a mother, I thought long and hard about the kind of adult I hoped my children would grow up to be. I wished for them to love God, to be honest, to treat everyone with dignity and respect, to work hard, and to always do what is right. It basically boiled down to integrity. So how was I to instill integrity in my children? It always came back to authority. My thought was if I never made them do what they did not want to do, then they would grow up to be adults who thought they didn't have to do what they didn't want to do. Images ran through my mind: adult lying in bed all day and then getting fired ("I don't want to go to work today"), unfinished college education ("I don't feel like going to class today"), etc. The "I don't want's" always lead to not doing what God expects of us—love one another, help one another—even if, and especially if, you do not want to. Sometimes I would give my kids options, but the outcome was always what I needed them to do. For instance, I would say to unload the dishwasher to which they might have answered that they had done it the last time. I would then say to unload the dishwasher now or unload and reload the dishwasher, and that would somehow get the original command accomplished.

—Carla

Biblical Principle
TRUST AND SECURITY

Parent Tidbit: Consistency builds trust and creates security.
Quip: "I know what's best for you."

You will keep in perfect peace him whose mind is steadfast, because he
trusts in you.
Isaiah 26:3

You probably don't need a book on how to love your kids and take care of them. God miraculously gave us those strong, natural instincts. But as our babies become toddlers and preschoolers, we can easily become confused as to what is best for them. Because we love them so much, it is easy to fall into the trap of just looking at their short-term happiness. But in order for kids to thrive, they need to trust their parents and feel safe and secure. Children must feel safe deep in their soul before your voice can have an impact on their behavior.

It is easy to make a newborn feel safe and secure. When we swaddle our newborn babies, it acts as a physical reminder to their brain of the physical conditions within the womb to make them feel safe and secure. But how does a toddler or preschooler feel safe? As the infant grows into a toddler, the child receives emotional security by knowing they can trust you to love them, take care of them, and do what is best for them.

Emotional rest and security is what we want for our children. We want them to trust that we know the bigger picture, that we have their good in mind. Just like God has our best in mind and plans to prosper us, that is what we also want for our children.

"For I know the plans I have for you," declares the Lord, "plans to prosper you and not to harm you, plans to give you hope and a future" (Jeremiah 29:11).

What helps create this sense of safety and stability? Consistency. Rules stay the same. Expectations stay the same. Rituals and routines stay the same. Each time a child experiences the same thing over and over, they learn to depend on it and trust that it will be there.

Establish rituals that pour love into your child's love tank. Once the child learns the bedtime routine in infancy, the child starts to feel safe. A calmness comes over him when he learns what to expect. Perhaps it's a favorite book read each night or a song sung after a snuggle time. These rituals create a sense of what's expected and that helps the baby or young child feel calm and safe. Develop little rituals every time your preschooler leaves your car, such as saying, "I love you to the moon and back" or "See ya later alligator." These rituals of loving expressions pour into the child a sense of safety. They feel valued and secured, are more able to thrive, and are also more able to withstand rebuke when correction is needed.

We have security in knowing that God is unchanging. His Word tells us that He is the same yesterday, today, and tomorrow (Malachi 3:6). We need to model this for our kids as well. Children are able to rest emotionally when they know what to expect. And when they rest emotionally, their soul feels peace. When children do not feel at peace, it causes confusion and more time is spent testing the boundaries.

There is no room for what I call willy-nilly parenting, or flying by the seat of your pants with no direction and no consistency. Willy-nilly parents allow kids to decide the schedule and routine—when to eat, when to get dressed, when to nap, when to have screen time, when to do homework. You get the idea. We cannot allow kids to just follow their hearts and dreams, because the Bible tells us that the heart is deceitful above all things (Jeremiah 17:9). As parents, our hearts can also be deceived making it difficult to recognize what is most beneficial for our kids. Stay in prayer and in the Word, so you are not fooled into giving into the whims of your child. When we parent from a wobbly standpoint, this creates instability and destroys any sense of safety that has been built.

We talked last chapter about the importance of setting boundaries so kids learn who is in charge. But setting boundaries and enforcing boundaries are two different matters. Enforcing the rules sometimes but ignoring them at other times creates an unstable environment for your kiddos. It is easy to get weary and to not follow through, but I encourage you to persevere and maintain! The easier route in the moment is to give in, but I encourage you to maintain and to persistently and consistently reinforce the boundaries and expectations you have set. When they push back, remind them that you know what is best for them and you have their best interest at heart. "I know what's best for you." And when your children aren't happy with the standards you expect, encourage them to take it up with God in prayer. It builds a foundation of talking to God and being in relationship with Him. When children are older and disagree with your boundaries, encourage them to bring their complaints to God. It teaches them to pray and have conversations with God.

When you don't maintain consistency with rules and follow through, kids don't know what to trust or whom to trust, and they will inevitably test you. God created all of us differently, so some kids arrive in this world more rebellious than others, often getting on our last nerve as they test us. These kids are desperately seeking strong, stable boundaries. Trust, obedience, and relationship occur once you've established stability through consistent enforcement of routines and rules.

Rewards and consequences are an important part of enforcing rules. As your child matures, you can add rewards for obedience. We all work for something—whether it's intrinsic or extrinsic, paychecks, words of affirmation, or status—and children are no different. Each person has a currency that motivates them, and it's up to you to figure out what speaks best to them.

Consequences are also important when training children. Success lies in knowing when to administer punishment and when to allow natural consequences to occur and in knowing each child and how they respond to various learning tools, such as time outs, removal from the situation, spanking, taking away toys, removing privileges, and grounding.

Be prepared for meltdowns. We all have our breaking points, and children are no different. Depending on the personality and even the physical state of the child, such as hunger or tiredness, some children might have more meltdowns than others. The key is making sure your child trusts you. Help them to feel safe, and you will see fewer meltdowns.

H is my child who deals with fears and anxieties. She started school at The P.L.A.Y. House at age three. It was a nightmarish beginning for all involved. The separation anxiety was extreme. There was much crying and not letting go. The solution was rituals and routines and consistency that finally made her feel that she was in a safe environment. The same person, my mom, had to take her to school and pick her up. In the classroom, she knew what to expect each hour she was there and she knew her teacher would give her strategies to cope and reassure her that she was safe while reminding her of their school routine. It did not happen overnight, but finally the tears and fits stopped. As she entered her pre-K school year, she walked in with great confidence. I cannot stress enough how having routines and consistency is vital for her, and I'm sure for all kids. Knowing what to expect and what comes next is crucial. She continues to need support with new experiences but has come a long way. We handle transitions together with constancy and consistency. I am thankful for all who nurtured her through those two years.

—Emily

RULES AND ORDER

Parent Tidbit: Keep rules and language simple.
Quip: "Always be safe and use good manners."

For God is not a God of disorder but of peace—as in all the congrega-tions of the Lord's people.
1 Corinthians 14:33

It's easy to overcomplicate things with our kids, and it takes intention-ality to keep things simple. For example, I focus on two simple rules: 1) Always be safe, and 2) Use good manners. I believe that everything involved within the confines of relationships can be rooted in these two rules.

When we make rules simple and easy to repeat, children are more likely to self-regulate and govern their own behavior as they mature. Modeling safety and good manners in the early years and labeling them as you go throughout the day helps set expectations. Toddlers repeat what they hear us saying, so we must say what's important and keep it short enough to have meaning for them.

Sometimes we get caught up in how smart our child is and how verbose he is, so we extend our discussions and explanations into lengthy lectures and mini sermons. This is a waste of breath and time— they have moved on and your words are lost and useless, so stick to short and sweet rules that you can repeat. Using the same few words makes it easier to effectively communicate to your kids and for them to recite back. You will need to repeat them over and over. Have the child repeat after you.

As I said, keep instructions short and sweet. For example, a child is approaching an electrical outlet or the stove and you yell, "Don't touch that." Some kids will freeze right away, but the more rebellious ones will want to do the opposite. Try this instead as you redirect the child physically away from the danger. "Stop. Always be safe. Is this safe? No! Always be safe."

Let them know that you want to keep them safe because you love them. "Why do we have rules?" "To keep us safe." "Why do I want you safe?" "Because you love me." This is a conversation you have to rehearse when they are very young. Repeat it in a game-style manner, or make it into a catchy tune—anything to keep it repeating and fun—all the while knowing you are laying a strong foundation for these rules.

Rules and boundaries present the perfect opportunity to tie it back to the Bible. Use few and intentional words to incorporate God's standards. "God's Word tells us to be kind. Is hitting a friend kind? No. Obey God's Word." Same scenario over and over. Be concise with your words.

One of the most common issues among young playmates and siblings is one child trying to take a toy from another child. Physical altercations can result from taking toys. Make children think about their actions by asking questions. "Was it safe to take that toy? No. Was it using good manners? No. God's Word tells us to treat others like we want to be treated. Good manners means treating others like we want to be treated."

Simple rules are vital not only for safety, but for helping your children build a solid foundation for relationships. Keep rules worded in the positive, focusing on the desired outcome, and keep repeating them over and over and over. Eventually the child will be the one repeating the rules, and the child will begin monitoring others and himself. Do not grow weary! Be patient with yourself and with the child. Be consistent and persistent with your concise rules and language.

Model safety and good manners for your children. Take advantage of teachable moments when you see rules not being followed at school or between siblings and other family members. While you're watching children's TV shows and movies, you can even point out rules and manners being practiced or broken.

> *E enjoys playing with his friends and siblings. Often, he will quiz them, "What's the number one rule?" He waits for a response and if there is not one, He tells them, "Always be safe!" I have seen him do this when kids are playing in an area that they should not be. He has commented to me about someone not covering their sneeze before as not using good manners. He shows his friends how to cough into their shirt to use good manners and not spread germs. He also has caught poor manners when his sister asked for something and reminded her to use good manners. His older brother has noticed that E is now displaying better manners himself. This is since he has language for the rules and has been practicing the rules as well as identifying them being used in our family.*

Biblical Principle
IDENTITY IN CHRIST

Parent Tidbit: Jesus meets our needs and then He exceeds.

His Love fills the hole down in my soul.

Quip: "You are a treasured child of God."

For he chose us in him before the creation of the world to be holy and blameless in his sight. In love he predestined us to be adopted as his sons through Jesus Christ, in accordance with his pleasure and will.
Ephesians 1:4–5

Most parents desire polite, well-behaved, happy, safe children, and I hope some of my tidbits will guide you in reaching these goals. More importantly, I hope this book encourages you to be intentional about guiding your little ones to Jesus and building the foundation for a lifelong relationship with Him. I take a holistic approach to reaching this goal, mindful that every word and action plays a role in developing their hearts and minds in establishing their identity in Christ.

What does it mean to have an identity in Jesus? It means to see yourself as God sees you—created by Him, treasured and fully loved, despite flaws and imperfections. Establishing an identity in Christ early on helps as kids get older not to believe worldly lies they will be tempted to believe about themselves. An identity in Christ also points them back to the Bible in every situation.

Identity establishes who we are and whose we are. When we were raising our girls and they would make a bad choice, we would often say, "You're a Holcombe and that's not what Holcombe's do." This was not to establish a sense of superiority or snobbery; it was to reiterate the standards of character that we had established based on God's Word.

In the same way your kids receive identity through their name, their identity should also be in the comfort of knowing they are a child of God. "You are a treasured child of God no matter what." Instill in them that they are valuable because of who they are, not because of what they do or the rules they follow or the achievements they conquer.

Having an identity in Christ means knowing unconditional love. Make your kids feel accepted and loved by creating an environment of unconditional love where they deeply trust that they are loved even when they get in trouble or when they express thoughts, feelings, and ideas that challenge yours. Although it's important that your kids follow rules and respect your authority, be mindful of not creating an environment of performance-based love. That's not how Jesus loves us. Modeling unconditional love to your kids will be part of their journey to Jesus. Separating the actions of your child from the value of your child is essential in modeling unconditional love. Let them know your love for them has nothing to do with their behavior or misbehavior, their accomplishments or their failures.

God loves us each fully and wholly, imperfections and all, and we can rest in the fact that we are His treasured children. Make sure your kids feel completely accepted and loved even when they misbehave, and teach them that God loves them even more than you do. As joint heirs with Jesus, our identity is aligned with Christ, and God sees us through the lens of His grace. In this knowledge, we find peace and safety.

If your kids can learn early on that they are valued, it can help avoid an identity crisis in later years. As children grow, things change—relationships, situations, activities, etc. Things will change, but God's love for them will not and does not change (Malachi 3:6). Let them grow up knowing that they are made in God's image (Genesis 1:27) and that they are fearfully and wonderfully made. "For you created my inmost being; you knit me together in my mother's womb. I praise you because I am fearfully and wonderfully made" (Psalm 139:13–14).

Teach them they are loved by God and made by God and are unique and special.

As Christians, we must know that our worth is not in who we are or what we do for a living, but in whose we are and how we live that out. We belong to God—we are adopted, we are chosen. We are covered in the blood of Jesus and nothing can snatch us from His Hand. That does not mean that we can simply do whatever we want. God has given His Word to abide by and obeying Him is for our good. When you know that you know that you know that God is good and that He loves you, then it is easier to be obedient to what He asks you to do and you can have peace in the middle of stormy circumstances, trusting that He is in control and is working all things out. This is mirrored in parenting when we communicate our love for our children. My mother always told me, and her mother told her, that there is nothing you could do or say or think or feel that would cause me to love you any less. I now say that to my own children. This helps communication to be open, as it provides a sense of security. When you are part of a family, you are set apart. My kids know without a doubt that we are all on the same team; that I am for them, not against.

—Melissa

WISE WORDS BRING LIFE

Parent Tidbit: The tone of your voice can kill or heal.
Quip: "Are your words helping or hurting?"

Do not let any unwholesome talk come out of your mouths, but only what is helpful for building others up according to their needs, that it may benefit those who listen.
Ephesians 4:29

The Bible teaches of the incredible power of the tongue. It can be used to either build up or tear down. If you want to learn more about what God's Word says about our words, I encourage you to read the books of Proverbs and James, as they especially speak about the power of our words.

The old adage, "Sticks and stones may break my bones, but words will never hurt me" is wrong. I'm sure we all have many examples of times where we've been hurt by the words of others, and, if we are honest, where our words have been hurtful. Our words matter. And because our words matter, the tone of voice matters! In his book, *The Five Love Languages*, Dr. Gary Chapman identifies one of those love languages as words of affirmation. I urge you to read this book and discover how words can be used to pour into the love tanks of your loved ones.

Using your words wisely not only helps show love to your children and enables effective communication but also models to them the importance of choosing words wisely. If you want your children to speak nicely to others, then ensure your language sets a good example.

Good, appropriate language helps children feel safe. Sarcastic language with young children, for example, teaches them that grownup's words have no meaning. For example, "I'm going to leave you if you don't come on! Bye!" I cringe every time I hear that one. The young child is now emotionally torn between doing what self wants—to stay and play or whatever the activity is—and going with you out of fear. Do you see where this could brew distrust or, at the very least, erode the relationship? Wouldn't it be better to simply state ahead of time that cleanup is coming and after that we are leaving?

We do not know how the toddler who is just beginning to develop emotionally is going to digest meaningless words of desperation or frustration. When we say what we mean and mean what we say, it builds those boundaries, reinforces the safety and security, supports respect and obedience, and grows the relationship in a healthy way.

The tone of your voice is also an important dynamic. When my girls were young, I struggled with anger that popped up without warning. I yelled when I was frustrated, in pain, disappointed, or angry. It was awful. I wish I could have a do over. Do not misunderstand me, there is a time and place to raise your voice, and your kids are going to make you angry, but yelling as a parenting style is not healthy. It does not build trust and does not allow for effective teaching. I eventually gave my anger to God and this Scripture became my mantra during that time:

> So here's what I want you to do, God helping you: Take your everyday, ordinary life—your sleeping, eating, going-to-work, and walking-around life—and place it before God as an offering. Embracing what God does for you is the best thing you can do for Him. Don't become so well adjusted to your culture that you fit into it without even thinking. Instead, fix your attention on God. You'll be changed from the inside out. Readily recognize what he wants from you, and quickly respond to it. Unlike the culture around you, always dragging you down to its level of immaturity, God

brings the best out of you, develops well-formed maturity in you. (Romans 12:1–2 MSG)

Nonverbal communication is just as important as verbal communication. Young children will sometimes look at your nonverbal language even more than your words, so think of your body language as an extension of your mouth.

There will be many times when you blow it and yell or say something you wish you could take back. I blew it more often than I'd like to admit. When my youngest daughter was about three, she would often ask me why I was mad. Often I was not particularly mad, it just sounded like I was. I would assure her that I was not mad, and then I would quickly change my tone of voice. Her young and innocent question held my heart and tongue accountable, and eventually I thought about how words would sound before I let them come out my mouth.

Not only do you need to be aware of the power of your voice, but your kids need to learn this awareness of their own voice. Kids get angry. There is nothing wrong with anger but anger becomes unhealthy when we use it to lash out at others. When you hear your kids yelling or saying mean things or using their words in any way that isn't uplifting, ask them, "Are your words helping or hurting?" Get them in the practice of asking this of themselves before they speak. Point out situations in real life and on TV where you see words being used for helping or hurting.

And remember that your children are listening to you all the time. It's easy to let your guard down when you're talking to your husband or to a friend and perhaps not realizing that little ears are always listening if they are anywhere within earshot. Are you talking badly about someone? Are you gossiping? Are you using appropriate language? "Pleasant words are a honeycomb, sweet to the soul and healing to the bones" (Proverbs 16:24).

As a parent of three children, it did not take me long to realize that they were all different, and that my goal should be to encourage and build them up instead of using language to foster low self-esteem, jealousy, anger, etc. My two daughters are complete opposites in all things. When they were young, they constantly fought with verbal attacks. I thought this was just being sisters. As they aged toward adolescence, the fighting became physical, and I knew I had to intervene. I called a "Come to Jesus" meeting one day. At first, all was quiet. I remained constant and quiet yet firm in my stand that we would use good and helpful, healthy words to get this settled. The grumbling and lack of affection had to change. My youngest daughter began to share first, telling how she felt a lot of pressure and expectation to be just like her older sister. She said she felt these unspoken expectations made her feel invisible and that she was having to live in the shadows. She recognized that she was totally different and wanted others to recognize this as well. This constant comparison had caused resentment and anger, and it had taken root in her heart. Teachers, family members, and even strangers would comment on the older daughter's physical beauty, and my youngest had heard the UNSPOKEN words of her lack of physical beauty. As soon as she began to share her heart, my oldest began to sob. As my youngest finished, my oldest immediately told her that she would trade all of her outward appearance for her younger sister's personality, warm and outgoing nature, and friends. Healing began to occur as they each shared from their hearts and realized that God had created them each differently for HIS purposes. Words of healing and helping flowed freely.

*—***Brandi**

— Biblical Principle —
GRACE AND FORGIVENESS

Parent Tidbit: Owning mistakes shows authenticity.
Quip: "Jesus forgives, and so should we."

Be kind and compassionate to one another, forgiving each other, just as in Christ God forgave you.
Ephesians 4:32

Whether you're a kid or a parent, there is never going to be a shortage of opportunities to apologize and ask for forgiveness. Kids mess up and parents mess up. We all struggle with the natural state of our humanity: selfishness, self-centeredness, and self-gratification.

Jesus went to the cross because God hates sin yet loves us. We are all in need of a redeemer. When Jesus said, "It is finished!" that meant the shedding of His blood fulfilled the redemption process. God is Holy. We can only enter heaven through the blood of Jesus.

We are all born sinners—selfish, self-centered, and self-seeking. As parents, it is our job to guide our children away from sin and toward selflessness. But our kids will still sin, just like we still sin and there will be ample opportunities for adults and children to practice grace and forgiveness.

As I mentioned earlier, do not be scared to apologize to your kids. Ask for their forgiveness when you mess up. I reacted in anger to my kids too frequently, and I learned to ask for their forgiveness. I am thankful God extends His grace to me constantly and that His grace never runs out.

When you apologize for a wrongdoing, not only should you own it by saying, "I'm sorry," but you should admit that it was wrong, ask for forgiveness, and offer restitution. It is so important to model a contrite heart in front of your children. When we can be authentic with our children, our transparency of owning mistakes and giving apologies strengthens the bond of trust between them and us.

And while it is important for parents to apologize with a contrite heart when needed, some parents swing the opposite way and apologize too often for things that do not require an apology. For example, saying things such as, "I'm sorry you're not feeling well" or "I'm sorry you spilled the milk" confuses the young child about the meaning of the phrase "I'm sorry." Instead say something like, "Please excuse me, I didn't mean to cause . . ." Be intentional in your word choices and only apologize in situations when you intentionally cause another person harm or pain. When you tell someone you are sorry, it should be intentionally and with great remorse.

Teach your kids to apologize when they cause someone physical or emotional harm or when they act wrongly. Make sure they specify what they are sorry for and then ask for forgiveness. This is also an opportunity to teach grace. Whoever is on the other end of the apology can learn to extend grace and to forgive the wrongdoing. And as with everything, tie these lessons into the Bible and to what Jesus did for us. Let them know, "Jesus forgives, and so should we."

> Bear with each other and forgive one another if any of you has a grievance against someone. Forgive as the Lord forgave you. (Colossians 3:13)

Each time you go through this apology process, you are showing them that we all need a Savior, we are all sinners, and that we all struggle with what is in our hearts. The flesh needs to be crucified, and in doing so, you lead them back to the cross of Calvary. The goal is that they ultimately recognize their need for a Savior.

Practicing grace and forgiveness to ourselves and others is a life-long process and comes easier for some than others. Start when they are young!

Miss Tammaney taught us many lessons. The one that stands out to me the most was a time that J needed to apologize, and he did not really want to. I was having a conversation with her outside after school one morning and he wandered off. I could not find him. When I did find him, he said "sorry" under his breath. This began a lesson that I will never forget and still use today. Miss Tammaney coached J in his apology. She said, "Repeat after me." It went like this: "I'm sorry" (Look your mother in the eyes). "I'm sorry (I have to hear you) for not minding and going where I wasn't supposed to go." "Better," Miss Tammaney said. Then she had him repeat, "Will you forgive me? I will not do it again!" This was all exceedingly difficult for J as I realized it would be for me. It meant taking full responsibility for his actions and looking into my eyes— the one he wronged. Asking for forgiveness takes an apology to a whole new level. We make it a practice to apologize like this still to this day. Thank you, Miss Tammaney, for having such a lasting impact on our lives.

—**Paula**

Biblical Principle
CONTENTMENT AND GRATITUDE

Parent Tidbit: Comparison is a thief that's real. He's after your joy to steal.

Quip: "You get what you get, and you don't pitch a fit."

I am not saying this because I am in need, for I have learned to be content whatever the circumstance, I know what it is to be in need, and I know what it is to have plenty. I have learned the secret of being content in any and every situation, whether well fed or hungry, whether in plenty or in want. I can do everything through him who gives me strength.
Philippians 4:11–13

Gratitude and contentment go hand in hand–a powerful lesson for parents and kids alike. God tells us to give thanks in all circumstances (1 Thessalonians 5:18). You will be amazed at the transformation that takes place with the practice of thankfulness.

When we compare ourselves physically, socially, educationally, etc., with others, we are robbed of the happiness in our hearts and we become discontent, always wanting for more, better, or different. This can become a vicious cycle leading down a dark path of bitterness, anger, greed, jealousy, and resentment. People will have a hard time achieving their God-given purpose if their eyes are constantly on self and what self has or does not have.

For kids, discontentment often rears its ugly head when they start comparing and thinking they got the short end of the stick—their brother got a bigger brownie, their sister got a better present, they didn't get to choose something. It is your job to teach your children to be content with what they've been given, situations they are experiencing, and the decisions made by others.

Parents, you can be tempted to give in when your kids aren't happy, but that is a disservice to your children. Kids need to develop the art of flexibility and acceptance at a personal cost or even a personal loss. So whether your child isn't happy with what you've prepared for dinner, with the restaurant chosen for lunch, or with the color of their sippy cup, teach, "You get what you get, and you don't pitch a fit." The child will learn that they are on the receiving end of the stick, and you are on the giving end. Tie it back to the Word of God, teaching that He tells us to give thanks in all situations. "Give thanks in all circumstances; for this is God's will for you in Christ Jesus" (1 Thessalonians 5:18).

Just as kids naturally compare what they have to others, we adults do the same. There will always be someone or something to be in competition with and to compare with. Stay away from it. Parents, do not allow yourself to get sucked into this trick of deception. Choose joy and gratitude.

Comparison is a thief that steals our joy. Sometimes we grownups use this weapon of comparison in our own lives and model an insatiable path of discord and discontentment for our children. If you find yourself always lacking, hungering for more status, finances, fads, possessions, etc., you are most likely modeling the same mindset to your children. When children witness gratitude in our lives, they learn to accept what they've been given. This leads to peace and contentment. Bathe your everyday language in gratitude for what each day holds.

Model gratitude with your own verbiage. Talk about the beauty of the day. "This is the day the Lord has made; let us rejoice and be glad in it" (Psalm 118:24). Speak about your happiness, instead of envy, over the accomplishments of others. Let your kids know you are thankful for them and for your other family members and for their uniqueness. Verbalize your thankfulness for the roof over your head and the food on your table. Express your thankfulness for God and for Jesus's sacrifice on the cross.

Parents, be especially thankful for your precious children and for who God created them to be. Do not compare them to each other. It is easy to fall into the trap of comparing kids' characteristics, struggles, choices, and learning methods, but instead choose to find joy in it all. It can be natural to gravitate toward the easier child while another one may be grating like sandpaper on your nerves. Change your mindset so that you're not comparing them; be intentional on focusing on each child's gifts and personality traits that you're grateful for.

Discontentment leads to restlessness causing us to lust for more of whatever . . . status, finances, fads, possessions, which all have to do with self. Humility is the opposite of this. When children are taught to accept what they have been given, whether it is a toy or a specific color of marker or a shortened playtime, they can also learn to practice good manners. These qualities in adulthood lead to peace and wisdom.

The saying, "You get what you get, and you don't pitch a fit," has become something our children are so used to that we have very few arguments over small things. Even now as our kids are getting older, we still use this philosophy when we need to purchase something for one child that the other child does not necessarily need. On the day of the purchase, we remind them that they get what they get. It is a mindset that the kids don't argue with because we have made it a part of everyday life from the very beginning.

—Mandy

ENDURANCE AND PERSEVERANCE

Parent Tidbit: Failure is a doorway—not a destination.
Quip for Kids: "Keep on trying, you CAN do it!"

Consider it pure joy, my brothers, whenever you face trials of many kinds, because you know that the testing of your faith develops perseverance. Perseverance must finish its work so that you may be mature and complete, not lacking anything.
James 1:2–4

Persistence and resilience are two lifelong survival skills that you have the responsibility to impart while your kids are still growing and developing. One of the best ways to instill these skills is by allowing children to accomplish things for themselves.

One habit I see happening in families today is the adult swooping in to rescue and help. It starts in infancy when a baby is trying to grasp an object and the parent swoops in to help. When the parent consistently completes tasks for the child, it creates a situation where the child has the inability to finish tasks, or worse, it creates an insecurity within the child about their abilities or intellect. As babies progress into the toddler years, parents tend to follow the same pattern and think they need to assist, whether it's helping kids put on their shoes, clean up a mess, or complete a craft.

Though there isn't usually any derogatory language in these types of situations, children absorb the negativity and the lack of respect, and over time, rely on adults more and more, becoming unable to do things themselves. This is easy to avoid: take the time to allow your children to persevere, whether it's formulating ideas, working out tasks, or completing manual manipulations and physical skills.

Each stage of a child's development actually has *work*, and this requires parents to allow time for children to do the work. When we rush in and, for instance, give the baby the object that's out of their reach without affording the baby time to do this work, we take away the child's opportunity to build the mental muscles of resilience and persistence. Over time, this erodes the natural desire to work, and our continued rescuing crushes the baby's determination and creates an unhealthy dependence on others for the child.

Children are unique in themselves and deserve the respect, time, and opportunities necessary for their growth and development. This should include lots of opportunities for practice and repetition and lots of time to fail at whatever they are learning—rolling over, walking, babbling, picking up food. The list is endless. Some of these learning opportunities, such as feeding themselves or washing their own hands, create messes. Don't say no to the messes and hinder learning opportunities that develop physical skills while also creating confidence, determination, and perseverance.

When parents swoop in and rescue, the opportunity for growth through failure is smashed and taken away, thus thwarting the needed practice for mastery. This rescuing and thwarting can happen over and over through toddlerhood. Parents do not realize their rescuing is setting their kids up for failure. When your children go to preschool or kindergarten, they will be expected to be able to perform certain life skills like putting on clothes and shoes, eating, communicating, etc. Will your child be ready? The same holds true for each stage of life.

When mom and dad act as helicopter parents, hovering over the child and leaving zero margin for practice and failure, the child is less likely to be able to do what is needed for independence at each stage of life. Later parents wonder why their child cannot keep a job and cannot "adult." The answer is obvious. The muscles of resilience and perseverance were not developed.

I have seen three years olds who cannot climb simple steps alone because they have never practiced. Their core muscles have not strengthened because they have not been given physical opportunities to climb and explore. Children who feel safe will eventually move through these challenges, however some children just simply shut down and give up. I often hear children who have been raised like this say, "I can't." When your child is trying and struggling and you are tempted to rescue, tell them, "Keep on trying, you CAN do it!" Show them you believe in them.

Encourage your young children in a non-hurried environment and demonstrate tasks. This means you need to create a lifestyle where you're not always in a rush. Choose not to live in the fast lane. Of course this doesn't mean life must be lived in sloth speed, but for the sake of the young child's development, make deliberate choices so that you're not living a hurried lifestyle.

There are many reasons parents hover over their children—fear the child will get hurt, lack of patience, a hurried lifestyle, inability to watch their child struggle, pride, perfectionism. (Read more about pride and perfectionism in the next chapter.) When we expect perfectionism from ourselves and our children, we set them up for failure. Our own OCD tendencies control our parental performance in certain areas. Our children see this in us, and it adds to the traits they may have inherited from us. We want the laundry folded and put up a certain way, so we do it instead of taking advantage of their enthusiasm and desire to help. Why wouldn't we want to capitalize on this energy and allow them to help? Just because it might take longer, or it might not be to our expectation? I can't repeat it enough: parenting is not about what is best for you, the grownup. It is about what is in the best interest of the developing and growing child.

Independence is more important than accuracy when children are in their early years. Does it really matter if the left shoe is on the right foot if he got the shoe on? If it does not feel right, then perhaps the child will learn which shoe goes on which foot. When the child's safety is at stake, then yes, step in and correct or immediately fix the issue. Other than safety, make yourself practice the art of patience and allow time in your schedule for the child to do chores, develop personal skills, and even choose words. Often we jump in and finish sentences or even anticipate the need. This takes away the opportunity for language to develop.

Remember the goal is a thriving and fully functioning adult contributing to his environment to the best of his God-given ability. The Bible tells us that perseverance develops character. "We know that suffering produces perseverance; perseverance, character; and character, hope" (Romans 5:3–4). Do not rob them the opportunity of learning to persevere and endure.

> *I had an "aha" moment the other day when I read a Facebook post about struggles. The meme went like this: "What if the struggle is the very thing God uses to grow us, to strengthen us, and build our character?" I had been hesitant about trying new playground activities that challenged his muscular development and strength. He was nervous about getting on a new type of swing at first and asked for help. I almost caved. I was in the habit of interrupting a lot of his learning opportunities by prematurely assisting but had recently been challenged to wait and encourage him instead. My mother was with us that day and she started talking him through it, whereas I would have also added the physical help simultaneously while helping. I almost robbed him of the pride of work well done and hindered his ability thereby thwarting his lesson in confidence and physical agility. He did the whole swing experience by himself and was extremely proud of his accomplishment! You should have seen his face!*
>
> **—Brittany**

HUMILITY

Parent Tidbit: The first place to start is to look in the heart.

Quip: "I'm not perfect and neither are you."

God opposes the proud but gives grace to the humble.
James 4:6

We are all born imperfect, even that sweet, precious baby you birthed! Parents sometimes set their kids up for failure by giving them the idea that they are perfect and overinflating their sense of self. Or sometimes parents can go the other way and put too much pressure on their kids to be perfect.

When adults continually use adjectives like "good," "perfect," "princess," "little man," etc., it builds up kids' egos and creates a false sense of self-importance. This puffed-up version of pride is the opposite of what God desires in our hearts. He desires humility. I believe that parenting took a turn for the worse when we bought into the psychobabble of the importance of building the child's self-esteem. The overuse of these shallow words puffs up the ego and leaves the child feeling devalued. These words are vague and have no basis for real meaning in their world.

Rather, try to edify and encourage your children with meaningful language. Be specific with words. "I really liked the way you picked up your toys." "God gave you strong muscles for moving your plate." "Your report card is awesome this time." "God made your brain to be smart, and you are making good choices in using your brain." Keep in mind that children do better with concrete language instead of abstract concepts.

Keep God in the forefront of their minds, so they realize all their gifts and accomplishments are from Him, so they develop confidence in who they are in Christ, and so they remain humble. It's easy to gush over our kids so much that we make them think they're perfect. We don't want our children to get big heads. Humility comes with the knowledge that self is not the center but rather a tiny grain of sand on the beach. The book of Proverbs is full of this wisdom.

Teach your child about strengths and weaknesses and the gifts God gives each person. Teach them about the characteristics of various women and men throughout the Bible. Acknowledge the traits and flaws of the people in the Bible stories so they can learn that none of us is perfect and that God loves us and can use us no matter what.

When you observe an area that your child is gifted in, let them know that those gifts are from God. When you observe areas your child struggles in, let them know that those are opportunities to persevere. Share your own weaknesses. It will help build authenticity into your relationship, while also teaching them that adults aren't perfect and that there is no unspoken expectation of perfection from them. Be mindful of how you react to your weaknesses and mistakes, since your kids will be watching. Use your mistakes and their mistakes and any bumps in the road as lessons for them.

Keep a check on your own heart's motives with parenting your children. It's easy to fall into the trap of expecting the perfectly behaved child, the perfectly good at everything kid, the perfectly well-liked boy or girl. You get the idea. Your child will pick up on your unrealistic expectations and take on the stress of trying to please you. Unrealistic expectations will never serve you or your child. Also take a look at your motives with disciplining your children. Are you disciplining out of pride to show others that you have a handle on your kids' behavior? If you have a strong-willed child, are you afraid of what others will think when the child is being difficult? Ensure you discipline out of a loving heart and from what is best for your child rather than falling prey to unhealthy fear or unhealthy pride in how the child's actions make you look or feel.

When we expect perfectionism from ourselves and our children, we set them up for failure.

My boys struggled particularly with striving for perfection. When they were younger, Miss Tammaney suggested we model failure for them. We would intentionally make a mistake— spilling a drink, making a simple addition error (something they could catch), writing something down incorrectly, etc. It could be anything that was wrong or that did not turn out as planned. We would simply clean up our mess or fix the problem without making a big deal about it or being upset and then move on. Today, they still prefer to be correct and do not like to fail, but the tears are considerably fewer, and we have embraced an attitude of "let's figure out what happened" and this has made the transition into the teen years much easier.

—Cindy

PATIENCE

Parent Tidbit: It's never too late to learn how to wait.
Quip for Kids: "What's your job? To wait!"

I wait for the Lord, my soul waits, and in his word I put my hope.
Psalm 130:5

How many times have you caught yourself impatiently waiting ... at the traffic light, a medical appointment, the grocery checkout, hairdresser? The list could go on. None of us loves to wait. Technology has made waiting even harder. Technology has sped us up so fast that one of my dear friends only listens to audiobooks on fast read!

What would happen in our minds and hearts if we rewrote those wait times as opportunities? Opportunities to pray, to listen, to observe, to be present in that very moment! Our stress levels would go down. Our cortisol levels would decrease. Our minds would be quiet, and our hearts would be calm.

We are taught that waiting is a waste of time or an error in efficiency, that it's an inconvenience to our own agendas rather than an anticipation of something good. As adults, we get caught up in schedules, deadlines, work, etc., and sometimes find ourselves impatient with circumstances and with people that we cannot control. Young children get even more frustrated because they have less control over these things.

A few years ago, the thought came to me to assign waiting as a job. During school that year, I had a particularly impatient group that liked to interrupt. I decided to make waiting a job. If a child would begin to interrupt, I'd say, "What is your job?" and then I'd say, "To wait!" We rehearsed this over and over throughout the day until the children knew the desired response and were able to answer it without my prompting. What happened to their behavior was immediate. After that very first time I started the drill, they instantly waited to speak. It was a God-sent instructional strategy that I quickly passed on to parents. This simple little moment of stopping everything and asking the child to wait shows respect for the child, validates what they have to say or do, and allows you more time to finish whatever it is that you are doing. It stops interruptions and teaches self-control, inhibitory control, patience, focused attention, manners, and, ultimately, submission of their will. When children feel respected, they will wait for their turn because they trust you. I went one step further and introduced the ASL sign for "wait" so that I could hold up my hand and give the sign while continuing the task at hand. This afforded less interruptions in our learning throughout the day as I was able to maintain the conversation at hand.

I give my students examples of things I must wait for, so they know waiting isn't just for kids. I, too, must wait to speak and not interrupt people. I tell them about normal everyday things . . . waiting in traffic, waiting for the brownies to be done baking, waiting for them to get to school, etc.

I believe if we can get the concept of waiting into our beings and pass it on to our children, verbally as well as a family lifestyle, we can make a huge impact into the next generation. God gives us a lot of opportunities to wait. In fact, Scripture teaches us a lot about it. Isaiah 40:31 is one of my favorite verses. It encourages us that our strength will be renewed when we wait upon the Lord. We read in the Psalms about waiting. These are a couple of my favorite Psalms about waiting:

> Wait for the Lord; be strong and take heart and wait for the Lord. (Psalm 27:14)

We wait in hope for the Lord; he is our help and our shield.
In him our hearts rejoice, for we trust in his holy name.
(Psalm 33:20–21)

If we can demonstrate this concept in our daily lives in front of our children, we increase the likelihood of it then passing over into their spiritual journey. As they grow older and get frustrated over waiting for God, be bold and share your personal waiting experiences with them.

When we wait on God, we heal, rest, focus, gain strength and courage, listen to His voice, and remember that we are not in control. Waiting reminds us of His sovereignty. In 2018, I discovered that the flu virus had traveled to my heart and left optic nerve and damaged both places. God put me in a big waiting room. I did not fear, but I did question why. The summer of 2019, God spoke to me through a song that used the analogy of a seed in the ground. The seed must wait, and while it's waiting it must surrender to the waiting. I have surrendered all of my "why's" to Him. I know He is big enough to take all of my questions, but I have reached a point that I don't have to ask why anymore. We all must wait.

Jeremiah 29:11 lets us know that God has plans for us. Often, we do not recognize that those plans require our lifetime to be fulfilled. We need patience to see those plans come to fruition. Sometimes life throws us in a tailspin, and we find ourselves in the waiting room of life looking for God's hand, His guidance, and His plan. We must wait. If you can teach your kids to learn to wait early on, it will serve them well into adulthood.

E had such a problem with waiting his turn to talk and now we shake our fingers and ask him what his job is! He always says to wait, though not always happily. It has been a game changer in our house. I used this in the bank recently. I was talking to the teller and E kept chattering. So I did the "wait" sign (shaking of fingers,) and asked him what his job is. He said, "To wait," then gave a little sigh and sat down next to me. Last evening, my mother, my wife, and I were having a discussion regarding plans for the home renovations, and E ran up to me saying, "Daddy, Daddy! I found a . . ." I asked if it was an emergency, and he said that it wasn't. I asked, "What is your job?" and he sighed and looked at the floor and said, "To wait." After that he waited until we were finished, and he could talk to me about what he found outside.

—Alex

REST

Parent Tidbit: An empty pitcher cannot fill a cup.
Quip for Kids: "God rested, so must I."

He makes me lie down in green pastures, he leads me beside quiet
waters, he refreshes my soul.
Psalm 23:2–3

I do not know if it is a female thing or a southern thing, but in my neck of the woods, it seems that women have the impression that taking care of self is a negative thing. Somehow an erroneous association between selfishness and self-care has been learned. In an effort to not be viewed as conceited and self-seeking, we go the other way and deny ourselves basic caretaking activities and time. But taking care of your own self is not self-centered or selfish. It is a necessity.

Be a good steward of what God has given you—your health and abilities! Taking care of yourself is especially paramount when you are a caregiver. If you want to give your child your all, then you need to take care of yourself. And if you want your child to learn to be healthy, you need to model good health in all areas. This includes taking the time to care for yourself, to rest, reset, and restore—good nutrition, exercise, sleep, friendships, time with God—whatever it takes for you to maintain yourself emotionally, physically, spiritually, and mentally. And remember the goal is ongoing self-care, not a one and done sort of super-charged battery event. As your child grows into each stage, your self-care can and should take on different forms and different lengths of time.

You deplete your energy when you are constantly taking care of others. No one has an endless supply of energy, nor can we store up a vat full to be used over and over. Instead we must create space in our daily schedules to replenish our own energy. God tells us in Genesis that He created us in His own image (Genesis 1:27) and that He rested on the seventh day (Genesis 2:2). If He saw fit to rest, then shouldn't we?

Don't be shy about telling your kids that you are taking care of yourself. "I'm taking care of myself, so I can better take care of you!" Do not let your kids make you feel guilty for taking a little time for yourself. It's healthy for them to know parents need time for themselves and that the world doesn't revolve around them.

We are a mysterious combination of three beings: flesh, soul, and spirit. Each of these have needs, and those needs must be considered. Our flesh needs water, rest, proper nutrition, and movement. Our soul needs friends, hobbies, and natural elements. Our spirit needs time with God in worship, in praise, and in His Word. When one aspect of you is neglected, it will eventually affect you, and, in turn, affect your family. Taking care of yourself is a vital aspect of parenthood, and when you skip it, you become exhausted in each of your beings: flesh, soul, spirit. And when you are exhausted, Satan creeps in to steal, kill, and destroy. He really doesn't care which part of you he takes from, and he will not only take from you, but he will also set up shop within you. Then other ugly things creep in, like bitterness, resentment, anger—all the qualities the Bible warns us about in Ephesians 4:31. Take the time to care for yourself so Satan does not rob your joy and open the door for these negative qualities to start to fester.

Naturally, exercise, good nutrition, and sleep will restore you physically. And it's not too big a mystery on how to fill yourself up emotionally and mentally . . . time. A bit of time away from the kids, some time with friends, time to yourself, time to take a bath or complete tasks. But time is hard to come by when you are a mom! I recommend having the support of a like-minded village. Your husband can help, but when he's not home or you want a date night, you need the help of others. The support of a like-minded village is essential in getting time to recharge and take care of yourself. As parents, you need physical support with the child as well as emotional and mental support. Parenting is exhausting even when it is good and the reason you are exhausted is selfless, sacrificial love.

Filling your soul is often the most neglected form of self-care. I encourage you to take an inventory of how you are feeding your soul. Are you spending a lot of time on social media? Do you have negative people around you? Are you watching a lot of news? What are you reading? Many years ago, I learned a saying that was very helpful in my mind's overhaul: Garbage in, garbage out. I challenge you to be aware of what is going in your mind through the media.

The best way to refresh your spirit is to commune with God, our Creator. Though it's difficult when you have young ones, find even a small amount of time to read the Bible and pray. Listen to Christian music. Be in constant prayer with Him throughout your day. Journal.

I've listened to Christian radio since my early parenting days. Focus on the Family and Family Life Today are two of my go-to resources for practical parenting help and also spiritual encouragement. I've also leaned heavily into the many resources offered by Nancy DeMoss Wolgemuth at Revive Our Hearts ministry. Making God a priority in your life means a lot more than Sunday attendance at church. If you are interested in insight into how to connect with God, I recommend the book *Sacred Pathways*, by Gary Thomas. It is an awesome Christian book that describes the nine temperaments God created in people so we can connect and worship Him in our own individual and unique ways. Properly feeding your spirit not only restores you but also models the same for your kids.

We all want to set a good example for our children but finding the balance between serving others and serving ourselves can be difficult. We must demonstrate self-care qualities to our children so they can learn how important it is for them to listen to their mind and body, so in turn they can have the spiritual and physical strength to care for others in the future. We as parents are in a way responsible for the future of our communities. One way I make sure to self-invest is to be intentional about having time with just my husband. Whether it is just dinner or attending a concert, that alone time with just the two of us keeps me going and reinforces the teamwork it takes to be parents. Our daughters look forward to their time with babysitters and ask when they are going to be "babysitted!"

—Stephanie

BIBLICAL WORLDVIEW

Parent Tidbit: Avoid the condition of culture's tradition.
Quip for Kids: "God's way is our way."

Do not conform any longer to the pattern of this world, but be transformed by the renewing of your mind. Then you will be able to test and approve what God's will is—his good, pleasing and perfect will.
Romans 12:2

Live in the world, not of the world. The Bible warns us about being worldly, which Merriam-Webster.com defines as "of, relating to, or devoted to this world and its pursuits rather than to religion or spiritual affairs." Opposite of being worldly is upholding a biblical worldview.

What does a biblical worldview look like in parenting? Grabbing on to God's Word first and foremost helps you to keep a biblical worldview, making the Bible the foundation of your mind and your heart, and letting it permeate your entirety. Although no one is perfect on this side of heaven, when you have God's Word inside of every part of who you are, you are able to better withstand the pressures that come from today's culture and yesterday's traditions.

I can't tell you what is worldly parenting and what isn't, and I'm not here to judge. The Word of God is the standard and the Holy Spirit is our guide. I think the different circumstances of each family have different repercussions, so it's up to each family to consider for themselves. But as with all parenting decisions, be mindful of the implications of your decisions. Keep an eternal perspective and a biblical mindset. Pray about what's right for your family and for your kids.

Just because the majority of people are doing something does not mean it's right for your family. This is also a good lesson for your kids. Just because most people are doing something doesn't mean you have to follow. Being counter culture doesn't mean automatically doing the opposite of the majority. It means remaining in prayer and not making decisions based on outside pressure.

For example, as your kids grow older there is an outside expectation to have them involved in multiple sports and activities. Before you know it, intentional and quality family time is conceded to the pressures of the overcrowded schedule of events and calendars, and both kids and parents miss out on what family has to offer. Suddenly there is no time for family dinners, no family downtime, no operating together as a family unit. Ensure your kids' needs for stability and security are taken into consideration when planning activities, and also ensure your needs for personal time aren't completely overshadowed by your kids' schedules. The right decision will look different for each family. Pray about it and don't just sign up your kids because that is what everyone else is doing.

As your family grows, so does the pressure to increase wealth and financial status. But go to God and pray about what is best for your family. I have seen dads step away from careers to stay closer to home and be present with their children more. I have seen moms leave the corporate world to provide the stability of home time. Please hear me. I am not saying that your life must be child focused. It is counterproductive to good parenting for the child to become the shining star and the center of all family attention. My point is to make prayerful decisions about what's best for your family, independent of what everyone else is doing.

Aside from wealth and time, culture also plays a role in the type of worldview we present to our kids. Society dictates that parents automatically embrace Santa and the Easter Bunny as part of tradition. As time has gone on, it's expanded to also include leprechauns, fairies, and elves. Yes, from an adult position, it is all fun and games, but you cannot predict how those words will settle into your child's core development. You may want to embrace these types of traditions or you may not, but before going with the tide, ask God what is best for your family. Consider how you can incorporate what your child will see or experience within the public and still maintain a biblical worldview. If the thought aligns with His truth, then keep it and act on it; if not, then toss it out. I encourage you to form your own convictions after you pray and seek God on this.

Decide ahead of time how you are going to handle cultural and family traditions and be committed to what God leads you to do. Going against the cultural norm takes grace, energy, and commitment. Doing this within your extended families will take respect, communication, and lots of grace. However, with God leading the way, you can do what He calls you to do. Remember, our job is to obey, that is all. He takes responsibility for the outcome!

We decided not to make a huge deal out of Santa. We are not anti-Santa or saying to look at him like he is the devil. We just act like he is any other Christmas decoration or silly, fun thing. Our middle child loves pretending and plays with one of those shelf elves that was given to us. He likes to hide it and scare his sisters. Our hope and intention is not to be dogmatic on this whole cultural issue, so they will not feel ostracized from society and won't feel like they have missed out on fun. As a Christian first and a mom second, I don't understand how we teach our children about Jesus—whom we cannot physically see and touch and who doesn't always give tangible gifts, yet who is very real and in whom we place our trust and life's decisions—but then promote Santa as a real person who will generally give you whatever you ask for. We set them up for confusion, and as a believer I know Jesus is not the author of confusion. Our goal is to put Santa in his rightful place—fictional and of no more importance than Frosty or Christmas lights.

—Lindsay

COMMUNITY AND TOUCH

Parent Tidbit: We're wired with a longing for belonging.
Quip for Kids: "God made us to need each other."

Two are better than one, because they have a good return for their
work: If one falls down, his friend can help him up. But pity the man
who falls and has no one to help him up! Also, if two lie down together,
they will keep warm. But how can one keep warm alone? Though
one may be overpowered, two can defend themselves. A cord of three
strands is not quickly broken.
Ecclesiastes 4:9–12

There's an old poem entitled "No Man Is an Island," which is a beautiful
sentiment that life should not be lived alone. Sometimes the idea of
becoming a hermit might be appealing when people are getting on
your nerves, but logistically living that out would be nothing short
of misery.

Through touch we first show our children that they are not alone
and they are loved. We all have the need to be physically touched,
hugged, and caressed. Even before that physical connection, there is
the connection within the womb, and the actual process of a vaginal
birth involves touch. Whether it's a vaginal birth or Cesarean birth,
babies need physical touch. Physical touch is a foundational need,
and our brains react chemically when we experience various forms
of touch. It is important. After birth, babies will suffer tremendously
if not touched. Some parents choose a family bed to maximize their
child's need for physical touch. Snuggle time, skin to skin with the

mother and father is of utmost importance to a healthy baby. This physical touch creates a safe haven for the child subconsciously, and as the child matures, they always feel safe in a parent's embrace. In an article published by Stanford University School of Medicine, Dr. Susan Crowe shares this: "During this time, babies experience nine instinctive stages: birth, cry, relaxation, awakening, activity, resting, 'crawling' (a shifting movement toward the breast), familiarization, suckling, and sleep" (https://med.stanford.edu/news/all-news/2013/09/the-benefits-of-touch-for-babies-parents.html).

As we grow older, some of us still have the need for a lot of physical touch, while others don't. But remember that young kids do. Whether physical touch is your love language or not, provide your little one with plenty of hugs, snuggles, and hand holding. Rub their feet. Caress their head. As they grow older, they may continue to feel loved through physical touch, or they may let you know they don't want to hug as much or hold hands. Of course, respect their requests, but when they are young, and until you know otherwise, don't be stingy with your hugs, kisses, and snuggles!

As children grow, their need for physical touch grows into an emotional need for touch—the need to be included and accepted. These emotional touches are not limited to the confines of family, but also include friendships, classmates, teachers, etc. Peer friendships and family friends create a sense of community. Understand their need for community, and encourage friendships with other children. Set up playdates and create an environment where they can find their village. And as they get older, be careful to not let friend time overshadow family time.

Just as your kids need a village to connect and have a place to belong, you also need a village. There is an old African proverb that states, "It takes a village to raise a child." Your village should be a support system for you as you raise your child and should also provide you with a sense of community. Your village should include like-minded followers of Jesus who can offer support as you parent. A church community is vital for you and your kids and an important part of growing in faith. It also teaches the importance of belonging to a body larger than ourselves. The book of Acts shows us the importance of doing life together in its discussions of the first church, which was very communal. They did life with each other daily, ate together, and shared resources.

Your village might change from one stage of your parenting years to the next as you evolve and meet new people. Find a person that is a little further down the parenting road than you and ask them to mentor you. Ask God to send you "village people." God sent me a mighty prayer warrior and godly woman when I was first parenting. I still thank God for her. She was the first person to actually pray aloud for me over the phone, in the store, and at her home. No matter where we were, if I was in need, she obeyed God and prayed aloud over me. Her words going into my ears went deep, penetrating my flesh and settling into my troubled soul and ultimately feeding my spirit.

The importance of touch isn't just for us but also for others. Make sure your children see that community exists beyond their home and their known environments. Let them see you open doors for people, pick up other's trash, speak to folks in the stores, take a meal to someone at church who is ill. Jesus touched others. He washed the disciples' feet (John 13). He took children in His arms and blessed them (Mark 10:16). He healed through touch. The woman touched Jesus's hem and she was healed (Matthew 9:20).

Likewise, be open to opportunities for supporting others. Offer to swap a night out with another couple. Or when you are in a new stage of life, help someone who is in a stage of parenting that you have come through. Serving others, even strangers, is a form of worship. It is God's love in action. Participate in mission trips as a family when your children are older. Serve on the cleaning team at your church as a family. Our American culture has lost the multigenerational approach to life. Doing life together with others seems to be on the decline. Perhaps the human tendency for independence has destroyed this interdependence with family members, friends, and church family. The need for a village is astoundingly apparent as I see families struggling with a lost sense of community.

Teach your kids that God made us to need each other. We need the support of others, hugs from friends, the handshake of our boss, the fellowship of friends and family. Lean into this for yourself and your kids.

I am a mom to two very different little girls. One is overly cautious, and even the smallest bump will cause a dramatic reaction, while the other casts caution to the wind, laughing while picking herself up from a fall. Two very different responses to pain, and yet when they need comforting, for whatever reason, they need physical touch: from me, another family member, or the adult in charge. I scoop them up and hold them tightly, whispering that it is going to be ok and asking where it hurts. It is amazing how that little bit of physical touch can magically make pain and fear vanish as if nothing ever happened.

—Lisa

Our village is extremely important in our day to day lives. We receive physical, logistical, emotional, and financial support from our tribe. Both my husband and I work outside the home and need the help of family and friends in transporting our daughter to after-school functions as well as after-school care. My people support me emotionally when I'm feeling down and out as well as cook for us when we are exhausted. I know that I am blessed by having such a generous and engaged community. It is like having a living, breathing personal guidebook in our lives that grows as we grow. It's all about human connection, and I thank Jesus for mine.

—Donna

CONCLUSION

Parenting is hard work and requires a lifestyle of sacrifice. It is inconvenient, painful, and often difficult. It can be gut wrenching, heart breaking, and mind boggling, with the potential for disaster at any moment. Yet it is one of the richest experiences God created. It is short-term pain for long-term gain. The difficulties pale in comparison to the deep love and joy that parenting brings.

Remember that it is a privilege to guide and lead your little ones. God gifted you with the responsibility of your children, and He is there to help you. Lean into His Word. Pray for your kids. Ask Him for guidance. Dedicate your kids to Christ, and recognize that He loves them even more than you do. And when things feel out of control, know that He is in control and that He is the one, true, and perfect God.

For your kids to ultimately recognize they need a Savior, keep God in your everyday conversations. Do not put Him in a box separate from your ordinary life. He should not only be mentioned at mealtime blessings and nighttime prayers but throughout the entire day. Make Him a part of your everyday teaching and conversations, so your kids will be led to a lifelong relationship with Jesus. This must start in the early years. Jesus must be a vibrant member of your home.

To raise Christian men and women of character, we must be committed to the journey of parenthood and to discipline our own hearts and minds. We must continually choose commitment to God over the rebellion of our hearts. "My son, pay attention to what I say; listen closely to my words. Do not let them out of your sight, keep them within your heart; for they are life to those who find them and health to a man's whole body. Above all else, guard your heart, for it is the wellspring of life." Proverbs 4:20–23.

Training young children starts with training our own selves. "Set your minds on things above, not on earthly things" (Colossian 3:2). It requires taking each and every thought, word, and action captive. Little ones are always quietly watching and listening. The last thing you want to do is to create a double standard, where your life's actions do not line up to the words you're saying to them. They will be confused, and they will always choose to follow your actions instead of your words.

Model Jesus. Model good behavior. Model kind words. Model following the rules and trusting God. Model submission, grace and forgiveness, perseverance, joy, sacrificial love . . . The list could go on.

You will slip and fail, because we all do, but thankfully we have a God who forgives. When you mess up, ask God for forgiveness, ask your child for forgiveness, and keep on persevering. We can ask for forgiveness because of His sacrifice on the cross. When you grow weary of sacrificing, think of our Father's sacrifice of His Son and Jesus's love for us.

Parenting is constantly balancing grace, mercy, love, discipline, and consequences for each child, because each one is individual in their personalities and needs. Only God can truly give that perfect sacrificial love, but we must model it to the best of our abilities to be good parents. We must be in fellowship with the Father through the power of Jesus in order for the Holy Spirit to display His fruit in our lives. It is a lifestyle—a race, not a sprint. Paul refers to the Christian walk as a race and to himself as an athlete. "Do you not know that in a race all the runners run, but only one gets the prize? Run in such a way as to get the prize" (1 Corinthians 9:24). Ultimately, the prize of Jesus and eternal life will be your child's decision, but it is your job to train them and set them up with a foundation that leads them to run the race and be on the journey with Jesus.

"And now these three remain: faith, hope and love. But the greatest of these is love" (1 Corinthians 13:13). Above all, love your kids. Love them enough to make those hard decisions that will lead them to honoring you and loving God. "Start children off on the way they should go, and even when they are old they will not turn from it" (Proverbs 22:6).

ORDER INFORMATION

To order additional copies of this book, please visit
www.redemption-press.com.
Also available at Christian bookstores and Barnes and Noble.